Food
JOKES

A Buddy Book
by **Hugh Moore**

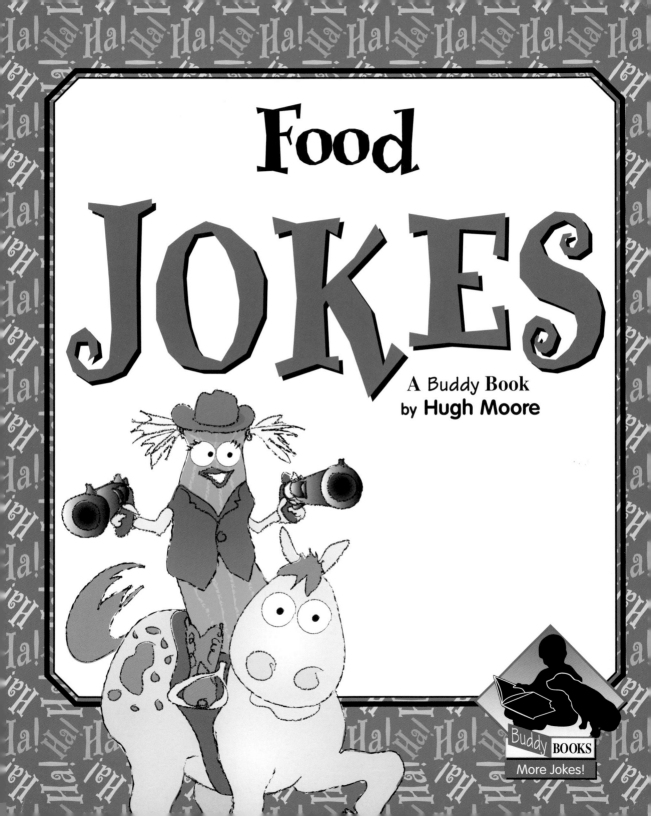

Buddy BOOKS

More Jokes!

VISIT US AT

www.abdopub.com

Published by ABDO Publishing Company, 4940 Viking Drive, Suite 622, Edina, Minnesota 55435.
Copyright © 2005 by Abdo Consulting Group, Inc. International copyrights reserved in all countries. No
part of this book may be reproduced in any form without written permission from the publisher.

Printed in the United States.

Edited by: Sarah Tieck
Contributing Editors: Jeff Lorge, Michael P. Goecke
Graphic Design: Deborah Coldiron
Illustrations by: Deborah Coldiron and Maria Hosley

Library of Congress Cataloging-in-Publication Data

Moore, Hugh, 1970-
    Food jokes / Hugh Moore.
        p. cm. — (More jokes!)
    Includes index.
    ISBN 1-59197-871-8
        1. Food—Juvenile humor. 2. Riddles, Juvenile. I. Title. II. Series.

PN6231.F66M66 2005
818'.5402—dc22

                                                                2004057512

What did the mayonnaise say to
the refrigerator?

What has ears but can't hear a thing?

A cornfield!

Why do fish avoid the computer?

So they don't get caught in the Inter-net!

Why couldn't the sesame seed stop playing cards?

Because he was on a roll!

What did the hungry computer eat?

Chips, one byte at a time!

What starts with "t" ends with "t" and is filled with tea?

A teapot!

How can you tell if an elephant has been in your refrigerator?

Footprints in the cheesecake!

What vegetable needs a plumber?

A leek!

What vegetable can tie your stomach in knots?

String beans!

When is a cucumber like a strawberry?

When one is in a pickle and the other is in a jam!

What do you get when you put three ducks in a box?

32 oz (without ducks)

How does the man in the moon
eat his food?

In satellite dishes!

Where does a bat eat his dinner?

On home plate, and he has a ball!

Why don't chickens play sports?

Because they hit fowl balls!

What did one knife say to the other?

Look sharp!

What does a cat call a mouse on a skateboard?

A meal on wheels!

9

Why did the tomato go out with a prune?

Because he couldn't find a date!

Why did the tomato blush?

Because he saw the salad dressing!

If you had five oranges in one hand and five pears in the other hand what would you have?

Huge hands!

Which veggie plays sports?

Squash!

Where do carrots go to sing on a Friday night?

To a carrot-oke bar!

What do sea monsters eat for lunch?

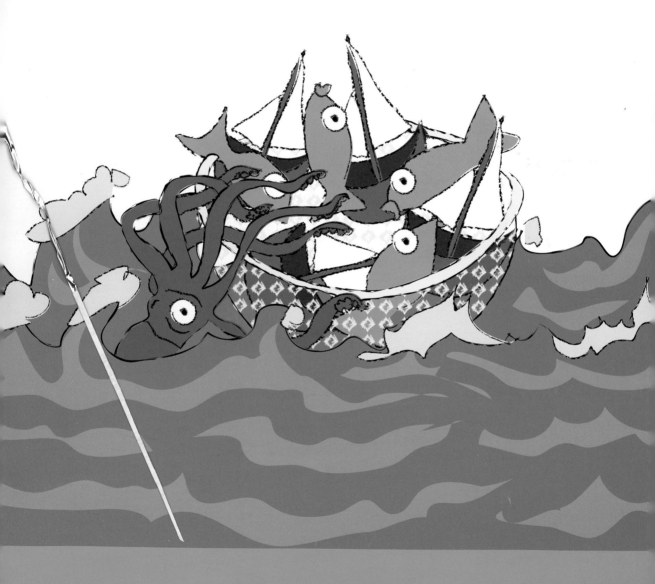

Fish and ships!

Why don't eggs tell jokes?

They'd crack each other up!

What beans never grow in a garden?

Jelly beans!

Which food is essential to good music?

The beet!

Why did the man pour veggies all over the world?

He wanted peas on earth!

What vegetable might you find in your basement?

Cellar-y!

Why do potatoes make good detectives?

Because they keep their eyes peeled!

What is Dracula's favorite food?

Neck-tarines!

Why is history like a fruitcake?

Because it's full of dates!

What is green and goes to summer camp?

What is green and a great trick shooter?

Annie Okra!

Did you hear the joke about oatmeal?

It's a lot of mush!

Why do you eat so fast?

I want to eat as much as possible before losing my appetite!

Jack: Would you like some Egyptian pie?
Jill: What's Egyptian pie?

Jack: You know, the kind mummy used to make!

Why did the man eat at the bank?

He wanted to eat rich food!

What did the mother ghost tell the baby ghost when he ate too fast?

Stop goblin your food!

What does the richest person in the world make for dinner every night?

Reservations!

What do you call a stolen yam?

A hot potato!

How do you make milk shake?

Give it a good scare!

Mike: I trained the dog not to beg at the table!
Shelley: How did you do that?

Mike: I let him taste my cooking!

What wobbles when it flies?

A jelly-copter!

How do you fix a cracked pumpkin?

With a pumpkin patch!

What is the most romantic fruit salad?

A date with a peach!

What is the pickle capital of the world?

Dill-adelphia!

What is the strongest vegetable in the world?

A muscle sprout!

What's in an astronaut's favorite sandwich?

Launch meat!

Customer: Do you serve crabs here?

Waiter: Yes, sir. We'll serve just about anybody!

Why did the man stare at the can of orange juice?

Because it said, "Concentrate!"

Why did the student eat his homework?

The teacher told him it was a piece of cake!

What's the worst thing about being an octopus?

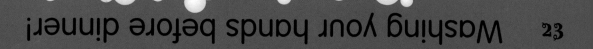

Washing your hands before dinner!

Web Sites

Visit ABDO Publishing Company on the World Wide Web. Joke Web sites for children are featured on our Book Links page. These links are monitored and updated to provide the silliest information available.

www.abdopub.com